Books by Edward Hirsch

Earthly Measures

Earthly Measures

POEMS BY

Edward Hirsch

ALFRED A. KNOPF   NEW YORK   1997

Copyright © 1994 by Edward Hirsch

All rights reserved under International and Pan-American Copyright Conventions. Published in the United States by Alfred A. Knopf, Inc., New York, and simultaneously in Canada by Random House of Canada Limited, Toronto. Distributed by Random House, Inc., New York.

Grateful acknowledgment is made to the editors of the following publications where these poems—some of which have been revised—first appeared:

Antaeus: "The Watcher"
Chelsea: "Mergers and Acquisitions"
Colorado Review: "First Snowfall: Intimations"
Denver Quarterly: "In the Midnight Hour"
Indiana Review: "The Reader"
The Kenyon Review: "Roman Fall"
Michigan Quarterly Review: "Devil's Night"
The Nation: "Scorched," "Sortes Virgilianae," "From a Train,"
         "Orpheus Ascending," "Posthumous Orpheus"
New England Review: "The Welcoming," "Earthly Light"
The New Republic: "In the Midwest," "The Romance of American Communism,"
         "In Memoriam Paul Celan," "Apostrophe"
New Virginia Review: "Nebraska, 1883"
The New York Times: "Summer Surprised Us"
The New Yorker: "Uncertainty," "Four A.M.," "Man on a Fire Escape,"
         "Simone Weil: The Year of Factory Work (1934–1935),"
         "Traveler," "Blunt Morning"
The Paris Review: "Away from Dogma," "Art Pepper"
Partisan Review: "Luminist Paintings at the National Gallery"
Ploughshares: "Pilgrimage"
Poetry: "The Renunciation of Poetry"
Raritan: "The Italian Muse"
The Southern Review: "At the Grave of Wallace Stevens"
Sycamore Review: "Solstice"
Triquarterly: "Orpheus: The Descent," "Unearthly Voices"
Western Humanities Review: "The Blue Rider"

Special thanks to the American Academy and Institute of Arts and Letters, and to the American Academy in Rome.

Library of Congress Cataloging-in-Publication Data
Hirsch, Edward.
     Earthly measures : poems / by Edward Hirsch. — 1st ed.
         p.   cm.
     ISBN 0-679-43070-9
     ISBN 0-679-43346-5 (paperback)
     I. Title.
     PS3558.I64E27   1994   93-26410
     811'.54—dc20   CIP

for Janet Landay

and Gabriel Landay Hirsch

The vulnerability of precious things is beautiful because vulnerability is a mark of existence.

SIMONE WEIL

Contents

1

2

CONTENTS

3

I

Uncertainty

We couldn't tell if it was a fire in the hills
Or the hills themselves on fire, smoky yet
Incandescent, too far away to comprehend.
And all this time we were traveling toward
Something vaguely burning in the distance—
A shadow on the horizon, a fault line—
A blue and cloudy peak which never seemed
To recede or get closer as we approached.
And that was all we knew about it
As we stood by the window in a waning light
Or touched and moved away from each other
And turned back to our books. But it remained
Even so, like the thought of a coal fading
On the upper left-hand side of our chests,
A destination that we bore within ourselves.
And there were those—were they the lucky ones?—
Who were unaware of rushing toward it.
And the blaze awaited them, too.

Four A.M.

The hollow, unearthly hour of night.
Swaying vessel of emptiness.

Patron saint of dead planets
and vast, unruly spaces receding in mist.

Necklace of shattered constellations:
soon the stars will be extinguished.

A cellblock sealed in ice.
An icehouse sealed in smoke.

The hour when nothing begets nothing,
the hour of drains and furnaces,

shadows fastened to a blank screen
and the moon floating in a pool of ashes.

The hour of nausea at middle age,
the hour with its face in its hands,

the hour when no one wants to be awake,
the scorned hour, the very pit

of all the other hours,
the very dirge.

Let five o'clock come
with its bandages of light.

A life buoy in bruised waters.
The first broken plank of morning.

Orpheus: The Descent

Two nuns selling raffle tickets in a kiosk
at the top of stairs stained with wine and blood.

The trains rumbling underground, a drunken
woman grabbing his arm and demanding money,

the odor of ammonia and urine wafting upward
to greet him. Unbreathable air. The strangled lungs

of a tunnel in August where turnstiles break
and teenagers shout into a microphone about God

the avenging spirit. Van Gogh's suffering face
wrinkles and stares from a torn poster.

The automatic doors, the wheatfields crack
and he stands in a car hurtling backward

through flickering shadows, swaying light.
In the newspaper at his feet the United Nations

debates a resolution, Muslims have the faces
of Jews peering through barbed-wire fences.

He closes his eyes and hears foghorns bleating
in a muffled light: oblivion claims him

across the bridge unlocking its steel shoulders
for a barge floating into the darkness . . .

The train stops and he descends. Soon
he hurries down a steep flight of stairs

toward an empty platform thickening with fog.
How does he understand where he is going?

My dearest: by the ache in his left side,
by the echo of sirens pulsing in the distance.

In the Midwest

He saw the iron wings of daybreak struggling
to rise over the warehouses stacked along the river.

Rotting wharves and bulkheads. Dead tracks
leading to railroad yards on the edge of nowhere,

the sun toiling in gray smoke on the horizon.
As if God had crumbled bits of charcoal

in the air and dusted the earth with ashes—
Eyelids of silt, thou shalt not open!

Scourge of asphalt and carbon, of slag heaps
and oil-stained piers, of soot and smog . . .

He was not a prophet of revision and announcement,
not the biblical kind, like Habakkuk or Amos,

and yet he wandered through the heartland alone
and saw the shattered spine of a bridge

collapsing in Gary; he saw the ruined breath
and gaping windows of a factory choking

in Youngstown; he saw the stench of history
seeping out of Sandusky and Calumet City . . .

Stops on the highway, stains on a dark map.
Foundries, industrial waste. Stripped quarries,

stripped land, what we've done to the sky
curdling over two drunks sleeping on an embankment

and waking up to a late day in the empire.
He kept speaking of Byzantium, of Constantinople.

He saw gulls feasting on garbage.
He saw the gouged bodies of the unborn.

Man on a Fire Escape

He couldn't remember what propelled him
out of the bedroom window onto the fire escape
of his fifth-floor walkup on the river,

so that he could see, as if for the first time,
sunset settling down on the dazed cityscape
and tugboats pulling barges up the river.

There were barred windows glaring at him
from the other side of the street
while the sun deepened into a smoky flare

that scalded the clouds gold-vermilion.
It was just an ordinary autumn twilight—
the kind he had witnessed often before—

but then the day brightened almost unnaturally
into a rusting, burnished, purplish red haze
and everything burst into flame:

the factories pouring smoke into the sky,
the trees and shrubs, the shadows
of pedestrians singed and rushing home . . .

There were storefronts going blind and cars
burning on the parkway and steel girders
collapsing into the polluted waves.

Even the latticed fretwork of stairs
where he was standing, even the first stars
climbing out of their sunlit graves

were branded and lifted up, consumed by fire.
It was like watching the start of Armageddon,
like seeing his mother dipped in flame . . .

And then he closed his eyes and it was over.
Just like that. When he opened them again
the world had reassembled beyond harm.

So where had he crossed to? Nowhere.
And what had he seen? Nothing. No foghorns
called out to each other, as if in a dream,

and no moon rose over the dark river
like a warning—icy, long-forgotten—
while he turned back to an empty room.

Devil's Night

He saw teenagers carrying flammable cans
of kerosene and boxes of wooden matches, torching
the discarded carcasses of Fords and Chevys,
spreading flames through abandoned buildings
and unused factories, lighting one-story houses
on narrow lots in small neighborhoods. He saw
old men standing on their front lawns in bathrobes,
holding shotguns and green garden hoses to stave off
the burning. A night of TV cameras and wailing
sirens, an hour of reckoning, moment of judgment.
He saw gas stations exploding like tinderboxes
and party stores being looted, and He understood
a new ritual of autumn, an annual reaping,
a fury that gathered night after night, until
it burst forth like a fever in late October.
He was one of the bystanders who waited
on the sidewalk passing a thermos of steaming
coffee and a bottle of whiskey, watching fire-
fighters wading into a furnace of buildings.
He was there when the blaze finally calmed
and the radios quit bristling with static,
when the exhausted crowd dispersed and drifted
toward home. And He was one of the few
who were still awake to witness the sunrise,
to observe a smoky disc flaring over the river,
charring the rooftops, glistening in the ruins.
He closed his eyes and saw darkness visible.
Yellow flames brimmed over cinders and ashes.
A broken skyline smoldered in the distance.

In the Midnight Hour

Once more the clock tolls like a heartbeat
in the church across the street and the bell
repeats itself twelve times in the tower.

Once more it is easy to think of you
staying up all night, in death as you were
in life, sprawled out on the floor

for hours at a time, drinking coffee
and listening to the Supremes, poring
over the pre-Socratics and the Neoplatonists,

looking up at the heavens. Who could
forget your first chilling encounter
with the infinite starry spaces,

with Cartesian doubt and numinous proofs
of the existence of God? Who could forget
your studious apprenticeship to the void?

Your sister described your apartment to me:
how the walls throbbed with the music
of the Vandellas and the Miracles,

how the lampshade tilted downward
and the curtains parted for the moths
banging against the window all night long.

Your father spoke in military metaphors:
how the cancer invaded your immune system,
attacking your pancreas, slipping unnoticed

through your bloodstream, setting up camp
in your bone marrow. He spoke of
chemotherapy as the body's last stand.

Your eight-hour shift at the Rouge Plant
working on a machine that manufactured fenders.
Your reading list: Wittgenstein's *Notebooks,*

Guide for the Perplexed, Waiting for God.
Your terminal song: "In the Midnight Hour."
But by then you were scarcely eating.

I remember the time when you suddenly
started talking about the membrane between
Being and Nothingness, joy and grief,

one tune and the next: "96 Tears" and
"Dancing in the Street," *The Consolation
of Philosophy, The Temptation to Exist.*

Student who once haunted my office,
bookish ghost who inhabited the classroom,
though it has been nearly ten years

since you passed from one realm to another,
I'm not yet reconciled. By now
there is a fault line between signifier

and signified, and the muse that appeared
to Boethius has become a principle
of uncertainty. Chaos is everywhere,

random and inexplicable. The self
is a construct of linguistic signs.
Proposition: God is a supreme ironist.

Proposition: God is a presence, indifferent
and absolute. Or else God is an absence.
Last night, instead of trying to sleep,

I conjured you up crossing the room
to the window and pointing at the moths
that seemed to want the flames so terribly.

Why? And where were they rushing?
That was something I wanted to ask you
before you disappeared into blue shadows.

I heard a barge wailing on the river.
I heard the wind lashing the branches.

The Romance of American Communism

The generation of Aunt Stalin and Uncle Pain
Believed in the glories of the Five-Year Plan,
The march of progress, et cetera, and so on . . .

How far away it seems: the new order, the slogan
Of History trudging the unemployment line . . .
Confess, confess: Aunt Stalin and Uncle Pain

Stood on streetcorners in the driving rain
Distributing pamphlets for Grandfather Lenin—
The New Masses, The Commune, etc., so on . . .

Statistics from Moscow, workers in the Kremlin,
The price of tractors and the cost of grain . . .
But the generation of Aunt Stalin and Uncle Pain

Was startled by the stories of Siberian
Camps: oh comrades of death, innocents of treason!
The bourgeois nature of regret, etc., so on . . .

In the end, it was self-loathing, self-recrimination:
A season in hell, yes, but the wrong season.
The sacrifice of Aunt Stalin and Uncle Pain—
The march of History, et cetera, and so on . . .

Scorched

It comes back to me as the enigma
of doorways and clocktowers, of standing
by an open window drenched in sunlight

and staring down at a drowsy piazza
where a waiter eternally cleans a table
and two cats squirm in the shadows.

3 p.m.: the hour of scorched absences,
the hour when the city slumps like a widow
and a dogged couple in their thirties

is forever trying to wring a child
from the clamor of each other's bodies
in a small pensione of the old quarter.

Look at them breathing against each other
in the hour of silences, the hour
of nothing violated and nothing affirmed,

of pleasure mixed with the fire of grief.
It is the wounded rite of infertility,
the inconceivable zero in the heart

of summer, the cancellation, the void
where what cannot be born is not born
and what does not exist will never exist.

Look at them cooling in each other's arms:
two muffled bells molded from the heat,
two bodies cast from the bright flames.

In Memoriam Paul Celan

Lay these words into the dead man's grave
next to the almonds and black cherries—
tiny skulls and flowering blood-drops, eyes,
and Thou, O bitterness that pillows his head.

Lay these words on the dead man's eyelids
like eyebrights, like medieval trumpet flowers
that will flourish, this time, in the shade.
Let the beheaded tulips glisten with rain.

Lay these words on his drowned eyelids
like coins or stars, ancillary eyes.
Canopy the swollen sky with sunspots
while thunder addresses the ground.

Syllable by syllable, clawed and handled,
the words have united in grief.
It is the ghostly hour of lamentation,
the void's turn, mournful and absolute.

Lay these words on the dead man's lips
like burning tongs, a tongue of flame.
A scouring eagle wheels and shrieks.
Let God pray to us for this man.

Simone Weil: The Year of Factory Work
(1934–1935)

A glass of red wine trembles on the table,
Untouched, and lamplight falls across her shoulders.

She looks down at the cabbage on her plate,
She stares at the broken bread. Proposition:

The irreducible slavery of workers. "To work
In order to eat, to eat in order to work."

She thinks of the punchclock in her chest,
Of night deepening in the bindweed and crabgrass,

In the vapors and atoms, in the factory
Where a steel vise presses against her temples

Ten hours per day. She doesn't eat.
She doesn't sleep. She almost doesn't think

Now that she has brushed against the bruised
Arm of oblivion and tasted the blood, now

That the furnace has labelled her skin
And branded her forehead like a Roman slave's.

Surely God comes to the clumsy and inefficient,
To welders in dark spectacles, and unskilled

Workers who spend their allotment of days
Pulling red-hot metal bobbins from the flames.

Surely God appears to the shattered and anonymous,
To the humiliated and afflicted

Whose legs are married to perpetual motion
And whose hands are too small for their bodies.

Proposition: "Through work man turns himself
Into matter, as Christ does through the Eucharist.

Work is like a death. We have to pass
Through death. We have to be killed."

We have to wake in order to work, to labor
And count, to fail repeatedly, to submit

To the furious rhythm of machines, to suffer
The pandemonium and inhabit the repetitions,

To become the sacrificial beast: time entering
Into the body, the body entering into time.

She presses her forehead against the table:
To work in order to eat, to eat . . .

Outside, the moths are flaring into stars
And stars are strung like beads across the heavens.

Inside, a glass of red wine trembles
Next to the cold cabbage and broken bread.

Exhausted night, she is the brimming liquid
And untouched food. Come down to her.

Away from Dogma

I was prevented by a sort of shame from going into churches . . . Nevertheless, I had three contacts with Catholicism that really counted. Simone Weil

1. In Portugal

One night in Portugal, alone in a forlorn
village at twilight, escaping her parents,
she saw a full moon baptized on the water
and the infallible heavens stained with clouds.

Vespers at eventide. A ragged procession
of fishermen's wives moving down to the sea,
carrying candles onto the boats, and singing
hymns of heartrending sadness. She thought:

this world is a smudged blue village
at sundown, the happenstance of stumbling
into the sixth canonical hour, discovering
the tawny sails of evening, the afflicted

religion of slaves. She thought: I am
one of those slaves, but I will not kneel
before Him, at least not now, not with
these tormented limbs that torment me still.

God is not manifest in this dusky light
and humiliated flesh: He is not among us.
But still the faith of the fishermen's wives
lifted her toward them, and she thought:

this life is a grave, mysterious moment
of hearing voices by the water and seeing
olive trees stretching out in the dirt,
of accepting the heavens cracked with rain.

2. In Assisi

To stand on the parcel of land where the saint
knelt down and married Lady Poverty, to walk
through the grasses of the Umbrian hills
where he scolded wolves and preached

to doves and jackdaws, where he chanted
canticles to the creatures who share our earth,
praising Brother Sun who rules the day,
Sister Moon who brightens the night.

Brother Fire sleeps in the arms of Sister Water.
Brother Wind kisses Sister Earth so tenderly.
To carry a picnic and eat whatever he ate—
bread and wine, the fare of tourists and saints.

She disliked the Miracles in the Gospels.
She never believed in the mystery of contact,
here below, between a human being and God.
She despised popular tales of apparitions.

But that afternoon in Assisi she wandered
through the abominable Santa Maria degli Angeli
and happened upon a little marvel of Romanesque
purity where St. Francis liked to pray.

She was there a short time when something absolute
and omnivorous, something she neither believed
nor disbelieved, something she understood—
but what was it?—forced her to her knees.

3. At Solesmes

From Palm Sunday to Easter Tuesday,
from Matins to Vespers and beyond, from
each earthly sound that hammered her skull
and entered her bloodstream, from the headaches

she sent into the universe and took back
into her flesh, from the suffering body
to the suffering mind, from the unholy breath
to the memories that never forgot her—

the factory whistle and the branding-iron
of the masters, the sixty-hour work week
and the machine that belched into her face,
the burns that blossomed on her arms—

from whatever weighs us down to whatever
lifts us up, from whatever mutilates us
to whatever spirits us away, from soul
descending to soul arising, moment by moment

she felt the body heaped up and abandoned
in the corner, the skin tasted and devoured;
she felt an invisible hand wavering
over the rags she was leaving behind.

Between the voices chanting and her own recitation,
between the heartbeats transfigured to prayer,
between the word *forsaken* and the word *joy*,
God came down and possessed her.

Sortes Virgilianae

(The Fortune-teller's Words to the Poet)

"I don't understand, I can scarcely see
In the faulty light, but I think he is standing
On a platform somewhere below the ground.

He is a shadow lost amid shadows, a wave
On the watery stairs, a shade tasting
The fetid air and touching the fog.

I see him taking a tentative step forward
And then another and another until the dark
Stumbles and welcomes him into its grasp.

Disconsolate being, a train shudders
In the distance overhead, and I remember
A wind whirling and spitting him out,

Steel doors opening and then clanging shut,
A branch glowing on the floor beneath the seat—
Untouched, forgotten. What does this mean?

The way downward is easy from Avernus.
Black Dis's door stands open night and day.
But to retrace your steps to heaven's air,

There is the trouble, there is the hard task.
And now he is wandering through a labyrinth
Of dead-end corridors and empty tunnels,

Broken mirrors and smudged signs pointing
Nowhere, voices echoing like footsteps
In the iron hallways. Listen to me:

If you want to become more than a shadow
Among shadows, you must carry back the memory
Of your father disintegrating in your arms,

You must bring words that will console others,
You must believe in stairs leading upward
To summer's resplendent, celestial blues."

2

Pilgrimage

Today I returned to see those two
Worn-out and rumpled representatives
Of the common world (were they mother and son,
Or did they merely resemble each other?)
Kneeling in adoration before the elongated
Mannerist apparition of the Virgin
Bearing a chubby five-year-old Son of God
Out of her sacred house and into the world
As she gazed down—calmly, impassively—
At those poor travelers who had journeyed
From far away to behold them, and to rest
For several hundred years in the dark
Cavaletti Chapel in the church of Sant'Agostino.

I dropped a one hundred-lira coin
Into a metal box and for two untarnished minutes
Of pure bliss I saw the light shining
Directly on the Madonna and Child descending
Toward the anonymous pilgrims glowing up
At them with unwashed, sunburned faces
And beautifully illumined, dirty feet.
I had come halfway across the world to observe
Those painted peasant soles filthy
From trudging over the countryside and through
The dusty, troubled streets of an unfamiliar city.

"Darkness gave him light," Henry Fuseli said,
And I thought of Caravaggio's street peddlars
And workmen, the thin prostitute in Piazza Navona
Who ascended the platform to become

A richly dressed Madonna in painting after painting,
That blunt tormented girl fished out of the Tiber
And used as a model for the exhausted Mother of God
In *Death of the Virgin*. How easily
She must have glided down the stairs as a child;
How desperately she must have tumbled
Into the moving black arms of the river at night . . .

And how gracefully the body of the Madonna
Of the Pilgrims—the portrait of a statue
Mysteriously awakened in Loreto—
Seemed to spring into life, how naturally
She floated over a shadowy wooden stair
With crossed ankles and radiant downward regard
For a ravenous world of pilgrims and travelers
Gazing up at her rapturously.
Maybe it was the hammered precision of the halo
Encircling her hair, maybe it was the uncompromised
Happiness of her features as she stood
Before the entrance to the sanctuary,
Or maybe it was the exalted innocence in her face—
But looking up at her looking down at us,
Peacefully, century after century, yes,
One could almost believe . . .

But then the light clicked off and the bodies
Dimmed into the shadows. I thought of those two
Peasants, satisfied but tired, getting up
From their sore knees and starting out
On the long journey home; I thought of the model
Lena stepping down from the wooden scaffold,
Clapping her hands and complaining that she was tired
Of holding a naked five-year-old god whose true mother
Waited patiently in the corner; and I thought

Of the painter himself putting down his brush
And turning back greedily to the theater of the streets—
A hungry sceptic again, a criminal non-believer . . .

Outside, a blue Fiat ground its wheels
And backed up onto the lower steps of the church.
Someone was shouting and throwing stones
Against a neighbor's window, someone was looming
Against an open bar with a switchblade sticking
Out of his pocket. Nearby, a teenager fumbled
With his girlfriend's blouse in the shadows
While two policemen paced by them, slowly,
Carefully, pretending not to stare.

To step out of that church was to step into
The city of Caravaggio, dangerous and impure;
It was to be dipped into the rough-hewn experiential
Pool of the world itself . . .
It was good to be in the open polluted air again,
Good to be moving down the white stairs onto the street.
I remember how the wind and the warm sun felt
Against my face, and how, as I hurried past,
I dropped a bill into the filthy outstretched palm
Of a gypsy woman with a rented retarded boy
Drooling in her arms, rolling her eyes and pleading
With a simple well-rehearsed grief that seemed
Half-feigned, half-real, and wholly human.

From a Train

(Hofmannsthal in Greece)

He saw tumultuous plains, interminable plateaus,
and the green breasts of a goddess withering in heat.

He saw the last road carved into a slope of Parnassus,
then into a petrified riverbed, curving between cones.

Ruins and more ruins, thousands of boulders scattered
like thoughts under the motionless pillars of a cloud.

Flowering hedges and broken columns, a cornfield sprawled
on its back like the Temple of the Gods, Delphi

and the Delphic Plain, the flat stretch of millennia,
stony cradle of a civilization that would not be rocked.

He saw two black rams butting on a peak, masses
of sheep cowering before the wolfish barking of dogs,

a young shepherd with a lamb slung over his shoulders
riding a red bicycle through a cypress grove.

All day villages sparkled and disappeared, like lights
fading on an open sea, or centuries passing,

yet a couple undressed in the next compartment,
a child slept, and twilight climbed over the mountains.

He saw fires of the Ancients flaring in a granite body,
Andromeda rising, a divinity that would not die out.

Unearthly Voices

(Hofmannsthal at the Monastery of St. Luke)

Wind tumbles the branches by the side of the road
and tiny clouds sail across a blistered sky.

Twilight in blue mountains, a bow-shaped valley
at the end of the world, one gashed pine

and a monk wading up to the waist in briar roses.
Here at last, dismounting, a worldly traveler

shakes off three days' dust and stretches his legs
on the eternal path. He follows a black gown

through a door carved into the mountain's flesh,
crosses an enclosed garden and enters a space

where a flame burns perpetually under the Holy Virgin.
Was this where the gods became the Lord Almighty?

He unpacks; he drinks clear water from a fountain;
he hears the unaccompanied voices of men rising

and falling inside a church, nearby but also far
from lamentation or desire. Why had he come

except to slip through the cloisters like a ghost
listening to Gregorian chants—signals from another world—

to smell the incense and honey that load the air
and contemplate the humility of kneeling

at Vespers, or lying on a stone-cold floor
in the early morning, or standing in meditation?

Why had he come except to prove to himself
that he could never be one of them? Suddenly

he hears a woman's tremulous voice glorying
from an open window, faithful, chanting,

and a second voice echoing hers, insubstantial,
as if the mysteries had borrowed a human breast

for singing, and then a third voice rising
beyond the others, a messenger whose flare gleams

over the walls of a darkened orchard, the cloudy
depths of a ruined city . . . The singing stops

and a smooth face appears at the window, a novice
whose hair falls across his shoulders to his waist.

The choirboys whisper together in the courtyard.
Tomorrow he leaves for Athens, but tonight

he is gazing at a thousand-year-old olive grove
that grows over broken columns, climbing the stairs

and standing on a balcony between two fig trees,
watching the evening star punctual over the mountains.

Now and then a light ascends, as if from water:
the shepherds keeping warm under a lonely crescent.

He peers into the darkness as into a cistern
and feels the centuries welling up beneath him.

An Unnamable is present, the Unreachable exists
in shuddering sheep bells and loud cicadas,

in dogs barking at each other across the hills,
answering questions, piercing the night's skin,

in stars blazing like torches, one by one,
on the earthly horizon. He lies down

on a cot—he will not sleep—and hears
churchbells flecking the snow-capped mountains,

far from home, somewhere near Delphi, and then
angels waking in the treetops, and owls calling

to wolves howling far away. Candles waver,
bodies flicker through the windy corridors

and soon they are praying and singing, kneeling
in adoration before an absolute presence, God,

the unfathomable One. He turns over and listens
to voices floating unearthly over the rooftops . . .

He drifts toward his family in another country,
almost in another century, on a different floor

of the dream. He broods: a stranger who visits
an ancient monastery is a tourist of eternity.

He believes nothing. He sees himself walking
on a narrow path, alone between bare mountains

while a single sparrow hawk circles overhead
and an icy stream threads its way underground.

He passes into the shade of a gigantic rock
as angels disappear into cypresses and stone pines.

The silence is wide and overwhelming, calm
blanket of oblivion, peacefulness of death . . .

At daybreak the voices begin again, ringing out
the darkness, bringing back the sun.

The Renunciation of Poetry

(Hofmannsthal in Athens, 1908)

These ruinous days of autumn. At dawn
the brightness seeps through the crumbling air,
at dusk the air gathers up the brightness.

So this is Greece, fabled decay. For years
he dreamt of caressing the flanks of these hills
and standing on the Aegean's thunderous shoulders,

but now he feels a gust of disappointment
at a country of tombs and columns, graveyards
and excavations, stones and fragments of stones.

The dust of travel still clings to his body,
and particles of sunlight fade on his skin.
What has happened to the eternal presences?

He climbs to the Acropolis in early evening
to watch the sun descending behind the Parthenon.
The first fires are being stoked in the sky,

and there is a smell of acacias, ripening
wheat and the open sea. But nothing penetrates.
In this light everything disintegrates into mist.

These Greeks, he wonders, what are they
but shadows dissolving into shadows, prophets
of non-existence, premonitions of emptiness.

Impossible antiquity, aimless searchings.
He despises them for becoming vain boasts
and eternal treacheries, wall decorations.

In the museum he sees showcases of death:
a goblet that resembles Kronos's shoulder,
a serpent that evokes the shape of an arm.

And then he sees her: an enormous figure,
heavy and lithic, staring at him
with slanting, expressionless eyes. A virgin—

animal, divine—a sacrificial offering.
He closes his eyes: someone is touching
her breast and kneeling, drinking her knees,

nestling a head on her foot. For once
the unattainable has opened its arms
and beckoned, the abyss has yawned . . .

He glances up: there are four others
glaring at him, vacant sockets for eyes.
Their voices are lamps fading in daylight,

an insolent laughter rising from the floor,
an echoing silence. Their faces are masks,
the overpowering bodies withdrawn to stone.

He turns back to look at her but she is gone:
the statue is dead, nothing can revive it.
The goddess is something that has died in him.

Roman Fall

I remember the bells of Santa Maria Maggiore
                    ringing on a crisp November morning
Under an undiminished blue sky
                    that seemed to go on forever
Over purple hills rising in the distance.

And I remember the rich unquarried blues
                    of the Janiculum at twilight,
The sky veined and chipped like marble,
The wind dipping
                    and soaring on transparent wings.

We were always stepping off
                    into the glassy Roman light
And moving back into polluted shadows,
Climbing the penitential stairs
                    and crossing under arches,

Sifting through cold smog
                    and unholy traffic,
Pointing at stone carvings
Of children dressed as angels
                    under vaulted domes and ceilings.

That was your last season as yourself,
                    the fall before your fall—
After that you were too sick and tired
                    to rouse yourself from bed, to travel—
And now, so many years after your death,

The past has the retrospective sheen
                          of ultramarines and aquatic blues,
The burnished clarity of wet leaves
                          falling to earth.
So many mornings the light pressed down

On the swollen eyelids of daybreak—
It was always raining
                          or starting to rain—
And the sun was a pilgrim straggling
                          over the seven hills.

Cold winds twisted up from the Tiber
And fog unraveled in the clouds
                          like a scarf of smoke.
At the Protestant Cemetery
                  the rain-driven winds

Blew across the names
                  that were written in water,
And at the center of the world
The Forum glittered like a lake of time
                  that had swallowed the ancients.

There were days when the sadness was everywhere
Like the gray light
                  that drizzled and pearled
On the cypresses and umbrella pines,
                  the eccentric churches and buildings,

The palaces lined up like wedding cakes
                  melting in the grand piazzas.
But there were also the nights
When the fiery oranges of elation
                  deepened over the rooftops at sunset

And the city was a net of stars
                          spreading out before us.
At those times it was impossible to believe
That a pale horse was already grazing
                          in the fields, waiting for you . . .

There was a cold morning
When Santa Maria della Pace
                          seemed to whiten in shadows
And an afternoon when we looked up,
                          as if casually,

At the stone eagles of the Last Judgment
                perched on Santa Crisogono in Trastevere.
I'll never forget how the sky shimmered
                          like a bowl of light
That poured over our heads as we climbed

One hundred and twenty-four stairs—
The steep unforgiving gray stones
                          of Santa Maria d'Aracoeli—
Built in gratitude
                for deliverance from the Black Death.

For me it all came down
                          to a solitary November day
When the sun was a bluish white flame
Burning overhead,
                a constancy in the sky.

All afternoon it shivered in front of us
                          like a bright summons
While the windows streaked
                          and flashed with light
And the wind tugged and pulled at our sleeves,

Pushing out at our shoulders
        as if it were going to lift us
(But only one of us was already
Preparing for the journey)
               into the radiance and beyond. . . .

The Watcher

(Leopardi in Rome, 1823)

He could not decide if the city at dusk
was the furnace of gods
                or the oven of man,
but he was there nonetheless, like an afterthought.

What was the world but an interminable afternoon
where sunlight smoldered
                and seared the rooftops
and heat clung to the skulls of churches?

Oracles lay prostrate in the blue dust
and shadows wandered aimlessly
                between the ruins.
Things that were once known were now lost.

He examined porticoes, columns, doorways
leading nowhere. Monuments
                to crumbling deities.
One-armed soldiers. Statues with broken genitalia.

A temple where vestal virgins were slaughtered
for letting the sacred fire
                flicker and die out.
If only someone remembered how to light it . . .

No one spoke to him on his daily outings—
a hunchback going blind,
                a walking sepulcher
climbing up and down the library stairs.

He was like a ghost radiating through fog.
And he was an eternal
                connoisseur of absences,
of tedious late afternoons in empty piazzas

and overheated nights in cramped apartments.
He heard clocks tolling
                from his bedroom at night
and felt the dull thud of the hours passing.

He watched a full moon lingering behind clouds
and saw a terrifying vacuum
                sealed up around him
like air strangled in the lungs of a tunnel.

Nothingness: the vacancies between stars,
the barrenness of a hilltop
                overlooking the arches,
the silence of a past that no longer exists.

Infinity: the distance beyond distances,
an impalpable unborn space
                glittering beyond time,
the bountiful emptiness of everything.

The Reader

It waited for him in the dusty treatises
On his father's bookshelf, in the back stacks
Of the local library, in the rare book room
And the manuscript collection on the fifth floor,
In the basement where they kept the well-thumbed
Periodicals and crumbling theology texts.
Unshelved and displaced, uncatalogued, overdue,
It waited in the background while he scanned
The entries and noted the citations, memorizing
The names of authors, writing down titles.
It shuddered when he read about the infinite
Starry spaces and the fast-moving river
Into which he would never step twice,
And it paused in the margins of the ancients,
In archaic Greek rituals and thunderous voices
Rising out of the whirlwind. He could not
Hear it breathing between the pages, belabored
In German, trilling in Spanish, stammering
Backward in Hebrew. He did not listen
To it crying out softly in the trees
Like a prophecy, though it waited for him
Nonetheless, a patient and faithful oblivion,
An emptiness, which he would not call God.

The Blue Rider

He remembered leaping over the corral
And riding on a blue horse
Through a blue valley flooded
With orange light in early morning,

The sky calm and unbending,
The sun shining with the glassy,
Transcendental clarity
Of high ceilings

In medieval German churches,
The radiance transfixed
Under the arches and glimmering
Through the rose-tinted windows,

But then the sky clouded over
And he woke up to a gangster moon
Pressed against the blurred windows
Of a train carrying soldiers

Over a bridge at nightfall,
The light blistered and bandaged
In smog, the blue horse gone
Into the flaming, war-torn mountains,

The sun crushed like a cinder
Under the metallic boots
Of twilight advancing,
A tunnel opening its black jaws

Over the glistening steel tracks
Stretching into darkness,
The wheels pounding, the iron
Hooves clattering beneath him.

The Italian Muse

(Henry James in Rome, 1869)

Thus was the past: hoary, formidable,
And lying about him in ruins,
In the imperial ruins of columns
("I found Rome clay and left it marble,"
Augustus boasted) and broken arches
Which gleamed under the celestial peak
Of a "characteristically antique"
Italian sky canopied with churches.

And here was the long-awaited sublime,
Encountered, as it were, in a hundred "views"
Of the past itself, the monumental laws
Of aggregated, immemorial Time,
Civilization's story—consequent, grave—
Peering at him with the exultant form
Of the Pantheon and the Coliseum,
Glowing from the other side of the grave.

He had harbored dreams of the "picturesque"
And now at long last he beheld it
As he looked down on a feudal street
Winding through the immortal city at dusk
(Eternally scenic, vigilantly Roman),
And here was that immersion in "Experience,"
In the uncrowned realm of physical sense
Which one deemed essentially *Italian*

(The operant word, he supposed, was "passion")
Even in that failing papal hour
When a shadowy splendidous figure

With two fingers lifted in benediction
Could still be seen, like an old-world idol,
Sitting in his coach by the Aurelian wall.
At times Rome seemed diminished, small,
Almost—he admitted it—*provincial,*

And yet it was but a ten-minute ride
Between one's well-rehearsed despair
And St. Peter's dome, that spectacular
Human achievement aspiring to God.
Or one drove out to "see" the country,
So bright and yet so intensely sad,
So full of the murmur of extinguished
Life, the flowering ruins of eternity . . .

He did not suppress the impulse of the moment
To go reeling alone through the weighty
Air and atmosphere of antiquity
In a virtual fever of enjoyment,
To descend into the maze of the Forum
And climb up to see the Tiber hurrying by
As swift and filthy as all history,
To stand at the very center of Christendom!

Thus Rome acquired the necessary "scope,"
A city of theatrical fountains
And Egyptian obelisks, Renaissance gardens
And the "churchiest" churches in Europe.
It was a modern city which showed
(And thereby was it inexhaustible)
A pagan shadow cast behind a medieval
Face restructured as a baroque facade.

One grew weary, of course, of "mere character,"
The swarms of one's addled fellow tourists,
Takers of advantage, beggars, priests,
The unremunerative aspects of human nature,
But there were also gods on every corner,
Stained Roman bricks crumbling with memories
Of indecipherable antiquities—
Latinity's stony mass and measure.

And here, too, were the landscapes of painting,
Seven fabled hills, and climactic gardens
Corridored with cypresses and pines
Opening their umbrellas in the morning.
He considered the Italian sun
A supremely irresponsible pleasure—
Decisively one could "waste" one's life here,
Ambling through the storied gates of tradition

With an aimless, amiable *flânerie*
Which left one free to follow every whim
(But how otherwise to "discover" Rome?)
And labyrinthine scruple of the city.
Where else were one's prodigious walks in line
With the perpetually transcendent attention—
Call it taste, fancy, perceptive emotion—
Of St. Ivo and St. John Lateran?

He was in the Protestant Cemetery
When he paused, finally, to brood upon
That trouble within trouble, the misfortune
Of death in an alien country.
The past was tremendously embodied
In Caius Cestius's pyramid,
But all he could think of was being buried
On foreign soil among the foreign dead.

Keats was interred here, so was Shelley—
But if it should "make one in love with death"
To lie there, that's only if death
Itself were conscious, a consequent clarity.
The place was heartbreaking in what it asked you—
In such a world as *this*—to renounce:
The resplendent light, the evidence
Of a solid blue block of perfect sky . . .

The injunction to the reader, on the tomb
Of Miss Rosa Bathurst, to lay down a wreath
"For she who lies beneath thy feet in death
Was the loveliest flower ever cropt in its bloom"
Struck him irresistibly as a case for tears.
"Here lies One Whose Name was writ in Water"
Was inscribed in stone under a broken lyre.
What *was* one to make of the advancing years?

That's when he turned robustly to the "world"
Where he was feted, introduced, observed
Contemplating the merits of the "local god"
With a pretty flag that had just unfurled,
And with her older sister, filled with verve,
Who was speaking about Venice in March
And the "craven" politics of the church.
One probed until one had exposed a nerve.

With a certain well-considered belief
He turned auspiciously from ancient Rome
And proceeded to Society's drawing room,
To the concatenations of current "life,"
To the excavation—in florid high relief—
Of that momentous moment in the life abroad,
Eminently social, wherein he heard
The passionate garrulity of human grief.

Traveler

(St. Lucia, 1985)

She wasn't prepared for the torrential rain
and unflagging wind,
                the laughable moon swaying
like a paper lantern over a chain-link fence.

She wasn't prepared for the "tropical" decor
of the hotel lobby
                or the crumbling wooden pier
or the tawdriness of things in the market.

Those hordes of noisy children following her
along the shore,
                that unruly one-armed beggar.
Outsize oleanders. Nosy fellow tourists.

She sat at a table writing postcards home
about the glass-strewn beach
                where music blasted
from cruise ships in the early evening

and the clouds thickened into darkness.
Ghostly afternoons sipping tea
                and munching cookies;
thunderous nights when lightning flashed

above the rooftops slanting in the distance
and trees huddled near
                the edge of the road.
Wild hibiscus knelt beside her window.

She saw herself folding a floral dress
across a cane chair,
                          turning back the sheets
and lying in a narrow bed far from home

where she counted sheep for hours on end
and felt the salt spray
                          clinging to her skin
as her body dissolved in disappointment . . .

She never expected to waken and find the world
intact, the sun prying open
                          the flimsy curtains
and flaring up—luminous, persistent, unabashed.

Orpheus Ascending

. . . like a penitent extending a flame
In front of him and stumbling backward through
A maze of tunnels, a miner rescinding his steps
And muttering because the walls verge on collapse.

He touches nothing, he feels the gases seeping
After him, acid yellows and sulfurous vapors,
Menacing fires of heat and dust. Somewhere
A doorway pulls and sucks him toward the light

And then he is standing above the dirt trying
To breathe the rancid air, smoke stinging his eyes,
Flames bursting from the open mouths of cauldrons
And furnaces. Is it night or day?

Human shapes, vague soot-colored figures
With fierce white eyes, are pushing wheelbarrows
Through the ironworks and slag heaps, shrouded
Forges and lime kilns, shafts and wheels . . .

Vegetal death, avernal air—where has he come to?
The ground has been gutted and ripped apart,
Its entrails smoldering and strewn everywhere,
Its skin pockmarked, covered with cinders.

No one notices him wandering in silence
Past deserted farmhouses and broken silos,
Touching the skeletons of trees, dilapidated
Stumps, pausing on the road to nowhere

And then lying on the parched brown grass
To think, to stare into a filthy haze and day-
Dream about a dog growling in the distance,
A vast explosion, and the deafening noise

Of cave after cave collapsing underground.
People are running and shrieking everywhere
And he races toward the entrance, but
The mine is sealed, there is no way down ...

Cavernous earth that has opened your lungs,
Let him sink into another level of the dream;
Let him return to the one he has betrayed
And face her body fading before his eyes;

Let him awaken to his own voice again—
Inconsolable Orpheus, who cannot decide
To sing, who never expected to find
A world above so much like the world below.

The Welcoming

After the long drought
                and the barren silence,
After seven years of fertility doctors
And medicine men in clinics
                    dreaming of rain,
After the rainfall and the drugs
                        that never engendered a child—

What is for others nature
                is for us culture:
Social workers and lawyers,
                    home studies and courtrooms,
Passports, interlocutory orders, a birth certificate
        that won't be delivered for a year,
                a haze of injunctions, jurisdictions, handshakes,
Everyone standing around in dark suits
                    saying yes, we think so, yes . . .

It has been less than a month and already
I want to bring you
                  out of the darkness,
              out of the deep pockets of silence . . .
While you were spending your fifth day
                      under bright lights in a new world,
We were traveling
            from Rome to New Orleans,
Twenty-three hours of anguish and airplanes,
Instructions in two languages,
                music from cream-colored headsets,
       jet lag instead of labor,

And on the other end a rainbow
                        of streamers in the French Quarter,
            a row of fraternity boys celebrating
                        in Jackson Square, the trolleys
                  buzzing up and down St. Charles Avenue,
The stately run-down southern mansions
Winking
            behind the pecan trees and the dark-leaved magnolias.

You were out there somewhere,
                  blinking, feeding omnivorously
                        from a nurse's arms, sleeping,
But who could sleep anymore
                        beside the innocent and the oblivious,
      who could dream?

How unreal it was to drive
                        through the narrow, twisted streets
            of an unfamiliar American city
            and then arrive at the empty bungalow
                        of a friend of a friend.
Outside, the trees waved slightly
                        under a cradle of moonlight
While, inside, the floorboards sagged
                  and creaked, the air conditioner kicked on
                        in the next room, in autumn,
            an invisible cat cried—a baby's cry—
            and roamed through the basement at 4 a.m.

All night long we were moored
                  to the shoreline of the bay windows,
                        to the edge of a bent sky
                  where the moon rocked
            and the stars were tiny crescent fish
                  swimming through amniotic fluids.

There was a deep rumbling underground,
And our feelings came in and went out, like waves.

By the vague tremors of dawn,
By the first faint pinkish-blue light
                    of morning rising in the east,
All we could think about
                was the signing of papers
                        in a neighboring parish,
            the black phone that was going to shout
                        at any moment, just once,
        our lawyer's slow drive to the hospital
                with an infant seat
            strapped into her car. You were waiting:
Little swimmer, the nurses at Touro
                didn't want to relinquish you
                    to the afterlife of our arms . . .

But so it was written:

On the sixth day,
After five days and nights on this earth,
You were finally delivered
                    into our keeping,
A wrinkled traveler from a faraway place
                who had journeyed a great distance,
A sweet aboriginal angel
                    with your own life,
A throbbing bundle of instincts and nerves—
        perfect fingers, perfect toes,
                shiny skin, blue soulful eyes
                    deeply set in your perfectly shaped head—

Oh wailing messenger,
Oh baleful full-bodied crier
                of the abandoned and the chosen,
Oh trumpet of laughter, oh Gabriel,
                     joy everlasting . . .

3

Summer Surprised Us

These first days of summer are like the pail
of blueberries that we poured out together
into the iron sink in the basement—

a brightness unleashed and spilling over
with tiny bell-shaped flowers, the windows
opened and the shrubs overwhelming the house

like the memory of a forgotten country, Nature,
with its wandering migrations and changing borders,
its thickets, woodlands, bee-humming meadows . . .

These widening turquoise days in mid-June
remind me of slow drives through the country
with my parents, the roads spreading out

before us like the inexhaustible hours
of childhood itself, like the wildflowers
and fruit stands blooming along the highway,

the heat tingling on my skin that would
burn with the banked fires of adolescence
and the no less poignant ache of adulthood

on those long detours through the park
during the last rain-soaked nights of spring
and the first beach days of the season . . .

It's the leisurely amplitude of feeling
that rises out of these expanding afternoons,
the days facing outward, the city taking notice

of itself after all these months, off-duty,
wearing short sleeve shirts and sleeveless dresses
the color of sunlight, the texture of morning.

It's the way we move toward each other
at night, tired, giddy after a day together
or a day apart, flush with newborn plans

for a holiday from daily life, in reality.
We are festive and free-floating. We are
poured out like a bucket of wild berries.

Apostrophe

(In Memory of Donald Barthelme, 1931–1989)

Perpetual worrier, patron of the misfit
and misguided, the oddball, the long shot,
irreverent black sheep in every family,
middle-aged man who languishes on the couch
with his head in his hands and often
spends the evening drinking by himself,
a dualist fated to deal in hybrids and cross-
breedings, riddles without answers, slumgullions,
impure waters, inappropriate longings, philosopher
of acedia, of spiritual torpor, nightsweats
and free-floating anxieties, sentencings,
sullenness in the face of existence, wry veteran
of the unresolved and the self-divided,
the besotted, the much married, defender
of the unhealthy and the uncommitted,
collagist of that mysterious overcrowded muck
we called a city, master of the solo riff
and the non sequitur, the call and response,
voice-overs and backtrackings, sublime bewilderments
and inexplicabilities, the comedy of post-
historical desires and thwarted passions,
first of the non-joiners, most unlikely,
tactful, and generous of fathers, you
who embarrassed the credulous and irritated
the unimaginative, who entertained the void
and recycled the dross, who deflated
the pretentious and deepened perplexities,
subject to odd stabbing rages of happiness,
weird bouts of pleasure, connoisseur of mornings,
of sunlight swinging into an open doorway,

small boys bumping into small girls, purposefully,
most self-conscious and ecstatic of ironists
who sang uncertainties like the Song of Songs
and dwelled in doubt like a habitation,
my wary, unreachable, inconsolable friend,
I wish I believed in another world than this
so I could think of seeing you again
raising your wineglass to the Holy Ghost,
your "main man," and praising the mysteries,
Love and Work, looking down at the weather
which, as you said, is going to be fair
and warmer, warmer and fair, most fair.

Blunt Morning

(July 15, 1979)

I'll never forget that morning when my mother-in-law
floated in a netherworld of morphine induced sleep,

those lingering hours of an otherwise ordinary Sunday
when she entered into a country that wasn't sleep

so much as a blue comatose state of semi-
consciousness that she inhabited to avoid the pain.

All that blunt sunlit morning we signalled each other
and talked over and around her emaciated shape

propped up on the pillows for what were obviously
her final hours of life on this earth.

She was breathing heavily, she was laboring
in her non-sleep, in her state of drifting

to wherever it was she was going—and suddenly
I couldn't stand it any longer. I moved next to her

and began talking, I didn't ask any questions,
I didn't know what I was saying I was speaking so quickly.

I said that we were all there, all of us, Janet and Sophie
and Susan, who was playing the piano in the living room,

that we loved her intensely, fiercely,
that we missed her *already*—where *was* she?—

we wished we could *do* something, anything,
that we each have tasks to fulfill on this planet

and her job now was to die, which she was doing
so well, so courageously, so gracefully,

we were just amazed at her courage.
I know she could hear me—

and that's when she opened her eyes and fixed me
with her stare. She wasn't moving

but she was looking me precisely in the eyes.
I'll never forget that look—haunted, inquisitive, regal—

and she was speaking,
except her voice was too weak

and the sounds didn't rise beyond her throat,
but she was speaking,

and that's when Janet and Sophie started singing
Hebrew songs—not prayers or psalms but celebratory

songs from Gertrude's childhood in Detroit,
and she was singing, too, she remembered the words,

except we couldn't hear any words, nothing
was coming out of her mouth, but she was tapping

two fingers on the side of the rented hospital bed—
and her lips were moving, she was singing.

That's when Sophie started telling stories
about their childhood, which seemed so far away

and so near, like yesterday, and Gertrude was nodding,
except her head didn't move, but anyone

could see that she was nodding yes,
and then Janet started talking about *her* childhood

in this very room
where sunlight burned through the curtains,

and then suddenly Gertrude jolted forward
and started waving her arms—

What is it? What is it? What is it?—
because she was choking on her own phlegm

and then she fell back against her pillows,
and stopped breathing.

Solstice

Remember how the city looked from the harbor
        in early evening: its brutal gaze
averted, its poised and certain countenance
        wavering with lights?

Remember how we sat in swaybacked chairs
        and marvelled at the brush fires
of dusk clear in the distance, the flames
        scrawled across the skyline

like a signature while currents shifted
        inside us? Ecstasy of fire-
works rising in midsummer, of fulvous sails
        flashing in the heat

and orange life buoys bobbing on the water;
        ecstasy of flares and secrets
and two bodies held aloft by desire . . .
        Judge us as you will,

but remember that we, too, lived once
        in the fullness of a moment
before the darkness took its turn with us
        and the night clamped shut.

Luminist Paintings at the National Gallery

Slowly the nineteenth century is turning into dusk
on Plum Island River and the Newbury marshes
where thunderstorms gather over Narragansett Bay
and the Boston wharves are tipped in flame.
Here is an exalted dwindling light going down
forever at Half Way Rock off the Marblehead shore,
at Norman's Woe and Camel's Hump, Vermont,
on the western ledge of Brace's Rock.

I suppose there is something strained
and oracular in these incandescent vistas
and glowing atmospherics, these salt rivers
and seashores masquerading as the letter S
(*The Sun, Serene, Sinks into the Slumberous Sea*),
the tides of Time rendered in magentas
and mauves, fiery violets and sharp new pangs
of red for rainy seasons in the tropics.

What is luminism but silence at Tongue Mountain,
a beacon shining off Mt. Desert Island,
reflections on Mirror Lake? It is melodramatic
coasts and marshlands, bleeding hillsides
and a dark radiance staining the canvas.
It is not light but a painting of light,
an exhibition of the body of light, a suffused
celestial presence, a void of wind and sea.

How far can our famous innocence carry us?
We are like torches at nightfall flaring up
and burning out under a streaked, transparent glass.

Crossing a bare common for the thousandth time
in snow puddles, at dusk, under a clouded sky,
Emerson said, "I have enjoyed a perfect
exhilaration. I am glad to the brink of fear."
I suppose there is always something suspect

and naive in American raids on grandeur,
and yet I like these local negotiations
between day and night, water, shore, and sky,
space and time. I like these intimate atoms
of color—cool, palpable, planar—that make me
think of towering bells in autumn
and organs booming in hometown churches,
schooners at evening lumbering across the bay.

Posthumous Orpheus

He wandered through a patchwork of open fields
And abandoned farmhouses, singing, but the rocks
Wouldn't budge and the trees refused to bend,
Rooted deeply in the ground, stolid, ungiving.
He sang with a grief that would have moved the land
If the land were listening to anything but its own
Hard processes, and he mourned with a music
That would have lifted the hearts of animals
Grazing in the pastures, except there were no
Animals to be seen anywhere, just a few scrawny
Crows scrounging for food. He sang of lost
Unstoried realms, of vows eternally broken,
His bride turning to shadows in the underworld
Because of him, but he never understood
That his voice was drowned out by the wind
Blowing incessantly across the Great Plains,
And by the steady hum of telephone wires
Stretching into nowhere, and by the whoosh
Of stray trucks whizzing by on the highway.
Eurydice was gone and there were no Maenads
To envy or ambush him, no one even to send
His head floating down the stream with a lyre.
The riverbeds were as dry as the brown wheatfields
And he was an alien among the pre-fab silos
And barbed-wire fences, the burnt grasses
Moving ceaselessly in place. No, for him
There was only the silence of a vacant sky
Deepening overhead, the glassy-eyed desolation
Of a flat, unforgiving landscape rolling on endlessly,

And the loneliness of a few scattered houses
Buried on the prairie. His seven priestly notes
Were lost in miles and miles of empty space,
And he mourned until he could mourn no longer—
A ghost of himself, of his own unheeded grief—
And then he gave up, defeated, and stopped singing.

Art Pepper

It's the broken phrases, the fury inside him.
Squiggling alto saxophone playing out rickets
And jaundice, a mother who tried to kill him
In her womb with a coat hanger, a faltering
God-like father. The past is a bruised cloud
Floating over the houses like a prophecy,
The terrible foghorns off the shore at San Pedro.

Lightning without thunder. Years without playing.
Years of blowing out smoke and inhaling fire,
Junk and cold turkey, smacking up, the habit
Of cooking powder in spoons, the eyedroppers,
The spikes. Tracks on both arms. Tattoos.
The hospital cells at Fort Worth, the wire cages
In the L. A. County, the hole at San Quentin.

And always the blunt instrument of sex, the pain
Bubbling up inside him like a wound, the small
Deaths. The wind piercing the sheer skin
Of a dark lake at dawn. The streets at 5 a.m.
After a cool rain. The smoky blue clubs.
The chords of Parker, of Young, of Coltrane.
Playing solo means going on alone, improvising,

Hitting the notes, ringing the changes.
It's clipped phrasing and dry ice in summer,
Straining against the rhythm, speeding it up,
Loping forward and looping back, finding the curl
In the wave, the mood in the air. It's
Splintered tones and furious double timing.
It's leaving the other instruments on stage

And blowing freedom into the night, into the faces
Of emptiness that peer along the bar, ghosts,
Shallow hulls of nothingness. Hatred of God.
Hatred of white skin that never turns black.
Hatred of Patti, of Dianne, of Christine.
A daughter who grew up without him, a stranger.
Years of being strung out, years without speaking.

Pauses and intervals, silence. A fog rolling
Across the ocean, foghorns in the distance.
A lighthouse rising from the underworld.
A moon swelling in the clouds, an informer,
A twisted white mouth of light. Scars carved
And crisscrossed on his chest. The memory
Of nodding out, the dazed drop-off into sleep.

And then the curious joy of surviving, joy
Of waking up in a dusky room to a gush
Of fresh notes, a tremoring sheet of sound.
Jamming again. Careening through the scales
For the creatures who haunt the night.
Bopping through the streets in a half-light
With Laurie on his arm, a witness, a believer.

The night is going to burst inside him.
The wind is going to break loose forever
From his lungs. It's the fury of improvising,
Of going on alone. It's the fierce clarity
Of each note coming to an end, distinct,
Glistening. The alto's full-bodied laughter.
The white grief-stricken wail.

Mergers and Acquisitions

Beyond junk bonds and oil spills,
beyond the collapse of Savings and Loans,
beyond liquidations and options on futures,
beyond basket trading and expanding foreign markets,
the Dow Jones industrial average, the Standard
& Poor's stock index, mutual funds, commodities,
beyond the rising tide of debits and credits,
opinion polls, falling currencies, the signs
for L. A. Gear and Coca Cola Classic,
the signs for U.S. Steel and General Motors,
hi-grade copper, municipal bonds, domestic sugar,
beyond fax it and collateral buildups,
beyond mergers and acquisitions, leveraged buyouts,
hostile takeovers, beyond the official policy
on inflation and the consensus on happiness,
beyond the national trends in buying and selling,
getting and spending, the market stalled
and the cost passed on to consumers,
beyond the statistical charts on prices,
there is something else that drives us, some
rage or hunger, some absence smoldering
like a childhood fever vaguely remembered
or half-perceived, some unprotected desire,
greed that is both wound and knife,
a failed grief, a lost radiance.

Nebraska, 1883

Westward the wagon jolted
                    along the ruts and trails,
along the interminable course of empire,
while the sun took a long time going down in the fields.

The earth was slow and hard
and there was nothing to see but land:
it was not a country at all
                    but the sketch of a country,
the material out of which countries are made.

She rode in the straw on the bottom
of the wagon-box,
                    covered up with a buffalo hide.

She rode until they had left the world behind
and she couldn't tell if they were lost
in the staggering flatlands
                    of heaven or hell
or some undiscovered region in between,

some middle country far away
                    from streams and rivers,
from Back Creek Valley
                    and the looming mountains of Virginia,
from quilting bees and church suppers.

This was the everlasting present without God—
the wind whistling across
                    a prairie without fences,

a prairie without trees or hills,
                    an undulating sea
of grasses that threatened to roll on forever.

She peered over the wagon at a sky
                          that never stopped waiting.
But what was it waiting for? And whom?

Every now and then a lark flew up
like a wild baton
                or a reminder of something
and then dropped down in the grass again.

If only she could keep from crying out . . .

Erasures, blottings, absences.
The punishing, unendurable distances
                        between one horizon
and another, one childhood and the next—
sod huts and dugouts
               carved from the Great Plains.

No, there was nothing out here
                  but the blankness
of the land itself,
            the vacancy of space,

a wagon sluing across the middle of nowhere,
and a nine-year-old tomboy—
               spunky, homesick—
doggedly standing up to the emptiness.

First Snowfall: Intimations

How long it has taken me to recall
That cold and radiant afternoon
                  in late October, 1959,
When twenty-five squirming bundles
Of trouble were subdued
                and then transfixed
By a bright snowfall that drifted
                and gusted like leaves
Outside the prison-like windows of Peterson School.

To us, it seemed as if someone
Was dusting off the rooftops
                and high ceilings of winter,
Dropping sheets of paper, wet and unlined,
From a cloudy, invisible sky
                just beyond our reach . . .
It seemed as if someone was painting
                and repainting the air
Until the day shined blankly, like a white wall.

While the teacher droned on
About positive and negative numbers
We were stilled by the absolute
                stillness settling around us,
By the steady erasure of lawns
                and houses across the street,
And by the hushed fragility of the trees
Glistening in the distance,
                ghostly, inhuman . . .

Our gaze moved upward against the white light,
But by the time we were released
Into the chilly, untouched
     otherness of the day
There were smudges and wingbeats
        floating in the treetops
And a long string of footsteps—
      the animals before us—
Crossing and crisscrossing in the snow.

Our cries shattered the stillness
       like panes of glass
As we stomped over the playground
And lay down on our backs—
      our spines against the earth—
To outline the figure of angels in the snow.
What joy we took in flapping our arms
        up and down, like wings,
And sinking down lazily into the soft ground . . .

It was as if the heavens had cracked
       and come floating down,
And I can still remember the giddy blankness
Of lying there and looking up dazed
       by the luminous crystals
Spiraling out of an opaque white silence . . .
But then we rose up from the ground, noisily
Brushing off our bodies,
     and raced each other home.

At the Grave of Wallace Stevens

(Section 14, Cedar Hill Cemetery, Hartford, Connecticut)

1

One thinks of the gods dissolving in mid-air
And the towering stillness of a cathedral at dawn.

One thinks of a solitary reader closing his book
In a ring of lamplight puddled on the desk.

Wind ruffles the curtains all night long
And the music of the spheres is silence.

Raindrops break the watery skin of ponds
And ponds are shattered mirrors of the absolute.

Stars are the white tears of nothingness.
Nothingness grieves over the disintegrating gods.

2

One imagines him as a prodigious morning walker
And a lonely metaphysician pausing in the park,

A rose rabbi, a sturdy man on a wide path
Dreaming of a sky washed clean by doubt.

One pictures him strolling under the umbrella
Pines and buttonwoods on the way to work,

Imagination's largest thinker conjuring up
Songs of human radiance twanging in the mist.

One thinks of him by the lake in a hard rain:
Mirrors on mirrors mirroring the emptiness.

3

We have stepped out into a summer storm:
Mute thunder and luminescent air, a wishbone

Of lightning turned upside down in the clouds,
A crescent of light poised on a dark steeple.

We have scattered sprigs of holly on the grave
And noticed the rosebushes blooming in shadows.

But we have not knelt at the heavy slab
Of Rhode Island granite carved with dates.

The ambassador of imagination is dead
And the guitars are silent. So farewell

4

To the maker of mournful summer melodies,
The connoisseur of moonlight, improvisation's king.

Farewell to the laudator of imperfection,
Grandeur in a business suit, the stylist

Of the void. Farewell to dried fruit
From California, tea imported from Ceylon,

And fresh ideas sailing in from anywhere.
Farewell to fidelity bonds and surety claims.

All those worldly realms of reflection
Have been traded in for a slope of trees.

5

The graveyard is carved into separate parts:
Streams and ponds, muddy paths, curving lanes.

You taught us to imagine the sublime
In a bare place, filling in the spaces.

Thus the sky is a lake brimming with tears,
The lake is a cloudy mirror. All morning

The wind rises and falls on transparent wings
And the traffic winding along Asylum Avenue

Is like a ghostly procession, a cortege!
The domes of skyscrapers gleam in the distance.

Earthly Light

(Homage to the 17th Century Dutch Painters)

1

I thought of northern skies flooded
with blue and gray, of monochromatic clouds
and rain-soaked wind blowing across the plains.

I thought of a cold day in March flattened
like unbleached canvas and steeped
in vertiginous greens, of industrious

local gods who furnished the low provinces
with rivers and lakes, waterlogged forests
and icy streams racing toward the ocean.

Or maybe there is only one God who supplies
the world with shorelines and sand dunes,
sunstruck mornings and thunderous nights,

maybe there is one God who keeps dividing
the world into water and land. I wonder
if the Dutch artists who could liquefy

sunlight and crystallize air worshipped Him
when they painted the large, whitewashed
interiors of churches; I wonder

if they were stealing supernatural light
or giving back to Him an earthly one
when they purified the sunshine skimming

grasslands and illuminating rooftops, burnishing
windows and mirrors, falling across floors.
If painting is to be a form of prayer

(prayer which Weil called "unmixed attention"
and George Herbert "something understood,"
one form among a myriad of forms),

then the Dutch artists prayed obliquely
by turning away from the other world
and detailing the plenitude of this—

the aurora seeping in from the sea
each day, the light dispersed equally
(was this the first time in history?)

on stout-hearted peasants and wealthy
burghers in irreproachable frock coats,
on civic guards and lacemakers, regents

and *regentin*, blacksmiths, cobblers . . .
Such a well-lighted lucky moment—
as if God had cracked the wooden shutters

of daybreak and started the scurrying
commercial hours that grew into weeks
and months, grew into the years.

2

"This brave nation lives with all it possesses
on a volcano," Benjamin Constant wrote,
"the lava of which is water," wherefore

everything had to be fastened down
and displayed before it floated away,
everything had to be acquired and caught

by those careful virtuosos of daily life
who belonged to the Guild of St. Luke
and painted flowers in terra cotta vases

and bowls of overripe fruit, who coveted
immaculate surfaces and imitated
the sheen on an iced pewter pitcher,

the sudden glow of a kerosene lamp,
a goblet half-filled with burgundy,
pages in a crumbling book of maps.

They were derided as "drudging mimics"
and "little deceivers," as "common
footsoldiers in the army of art,"

but they never ceased preserving and
rearranging a world of fish markets,
drapers' shops, brothels, dance halls.

The summer days swelled like good fortune
and they walked on well-scoured sidewalks
and stared admiringly at gabled roofs

and touched brick walls baking in the sun.
They were artisans who spent entire days
tracing the radiant afternoon light,

outlining the daily pleasures and sufferings
of usual people, the Saturday nights
and Sunday mornings of human life—

a wedding feast, a village kermis.
Naturally God was invoked and addressed
in sermons calling for gratitude and charity;

naturally He was remembered and then ignored
while the days slowly began to fade,
the taverns filled with revellers,

and the painters continued to record
a new country's ruddy complexion
and only slightly surprised expression,

its slashed sleeves and plumed hats,
its prosperous, secure, vanishing
bourgeois moment in the sun.

3

The market and tavern scenes survive,
conversation pieces, kitchen sagas,
a drawing room holding its breath

on a Sunday afternoon in late October;
what has lasted are sumptuous tapestries
and silks that you can *see* rustling,

spiral staircases and Persian carpets,
the texture of the world reduced and glittering
on fresh maps hanging in the background.

There's a woman playing the theorbo
for two suitors, a girl in white
sitting confidently at the virginal,

a family making music for themselves
while the light slants through the window
and trees begin to tremble in the cold.

Because there's also a goldfinch chained
to its perch, a pregnant woman standing
in the window frame tearing up a letter,

an old man grinding pigments. The colors glow.
And who remembers the inhabitants
of the leper colony and the poorhouse?

Who remembers the cost of too much work
in cold studios, mounting debts
and miserly commissions, paintings

traded for clothes and groceries, drawings
bartered for drinks at the nearest tavern?
Who remembers the untalented apprentices?

What has survived are the household bonds,
flowers, oysters, lemons, flies,
scrupulous renderings of credible life.

And who else painted for posterity
such profiles of human comfort and wealth:
all those pearl earrings and lace collars,

the horn of plenty blowing in autumn
for the ships gliding into safe harbor
with spices and perfumes from the East?

Travelers are marvelling at the paintings
displayed in every stall at the fair,
but look at that self-portrait of the artist:

what a terrible old man! Lines
have been chiselled into his face
and his eyes are burning.

4

I remember the warm day in winter
when I stood on a hotel balcony listening
to bells ringing in the distance.

I had just seen all those galleries
of seventeenth-century light slipping
through interior courtyards and alleys,

branding doors and ceilings, pressing down
lightly on the skulls of buildings.
I had just seen rhetorics of light flashing

on curtains and tablecloths, mirrors
and windows, old maps and well-preserved
canvases varnished and framed.

I was alone, and for a while I stared
into a sky washed clean by rain,
an atmosphere luminous and polished,

ready to ascend, transparent as wings.
I saw tugboats pulling heavy barges
up and down the ice-filled river

while a white disc flamed overhead
and bands of purple light that resembled
bruises drifted and gradually dispersed.

I thought of northern skies flooded
with blue and gray, of monochromatic clouds
and rain-soaked wind blowing across the plains.

I thought of a landscape flattened
like unbleached canvas and steeped
in vertiginous greens, of the artists

who could liquefy thickest sunlight,
and the tangible, earth-colored country
that was all there would be to paint.

That February day I looked directly
into a wintry, invisible world
and that was when I turned away

from the God or gods I had wanted
so long and so much to believe in.
That was when I hurried down the stairs

into a street already crowded with people.
Because this world, too, needs our unmixed
attention, because it is not heaven

but earth that needs us, because
it is only earth—limited, sensuous
earth that is so fleeting, so real.

Notes

"Four A.M.": The title and several of the images derive from the contemporary Polish poet Wislawa Szymborska.

"Devil's Night" is set in Detroit on October 30th. A tradition of looting and setting fires has developed there on the night before Halloween. The phrase "darkness visible" comes from Satan's vision of his own "dismal Situation" in Hell in Book I of *Paradise Lost.*

"In the Midnight Hour" is the title of a Wilson Pickett song. The songs "96 Tears" by Question Mark and the Mysterians, and "Dancing in the Street" by Martha and the Vandellas parallel Boethius's *The Consolation of Philosophy* and E. M. Cioran's *The Temptation to Exist.*

"The Romance of American Communism" uses the title of a book by Vivian Gornick (1977).

"In Memoriam Paul Celan" is structured after Celan's elegy "In Memoriam Paul Eluard." Paul Celan was the pseudonym of Paul Ancel, who was born in Romanian Bukovina in 1920. He committed suicide in Paris in 1970.

"Simone Weil: The Year of Factory Work (1934–1935)": During this period Simone Weil worked as a manual laborer in the Renault, Alsthom, and Forges de Basse-Indres factories in Paris. The experience was one of the gravest and most shattering in her short life (1909–1943). "That contact with affliction had killed my youth," she wrote in her "Spiritual Autobiography" (*Waiting for God*, posthumously published in 1951).

Weil described and meditated on her factory experiences in a series of letters, journal entries, and notes posthumously collected in *La Condition Ouvrière* (1951). The title of my poem and some background information are gleaned from chapter eight of her friend Simone Pétrement's biography, *Simone Weil: A Life* (1976). The logical propositions are quoted from Weil's essay "The Mysticism of Work" (*Gravity and Grace*, 1952).

"Away from Dogma": In her "Spiritual Autobiography," a letter addressed to her friend Father Perrin, Weil writes: "Keeping away from dogma in this way, I was prevented by a sort of shame from going into churches, though I like being in them." She goes on to describe her three crucial contacts with Catholicism (*Waiting for God*).

"Sortes Virgilianae": The title refers to the ancient practice of fortune-telling by choosing at random a passage from Virgil's poetry. What the fortune-teller sees—the substance of the poem—is an Aeneas-like figure trying to make his way through the underworld. The italicized lines, whereby the Cumaean Sibyl speaks to Aeneas from the mouth of the cave, are from Book VI of Robert Fitzgerald's translation of the *Aeneid* (1983), though I have modified the last phrase. The final six lines encapsulate an oblique ars poetica.

"Pilgrimage": The poem describes the *Madonna di Loreto* (sometimes called the *Madonna dei Pelligrini*) by Caravaggio (1573–1610). In Lecture II (1801) the artist Henry Fuseli claimed, "No painter ever painted his own mind so forcibly as Michael Angelo Amerigi, surnamed Il Caravaggio. To none nature ever set limits with a more decided hand. Darkness gave him light; into his melancholy cell light stole only with a pale reluctant ray, or broke on it, as flashes on a stormy night."

"From a Train," "Unearthly Voices," "The Renunciation of Poetry": Hugo von Hofmannsthal (1874–1929) wrote all his lyrical poetry before he was 26 years old. He then abandoned poetry and concentrated on essays, prose fiction, and plays. He also collaborated with the composer Richard Strauss on six operas, including *Der Rosenkavalier* (1911). Hofmannsthal traveled to Greece in 1908 with his friends Count Kessler and the French sculptor Maillol. My poems derive most immediately from his three-part essay "Moments in Greece," especially Part I, "The Monastery of St. Luke," and Part III, "The Statues" (*Selected Prose*, 1952). The reader may find it useful to think of the poems as a triptych that progresses from the moment divinity asserts itself to the historic instant when the gods turn into a single God to the time when divinity seeps out of tangible things.

"The Watcher": Giacomo Leopardi (1798–1837), perhaps the most classically learned poet of the 19th century, referred to himself as "a walking sepulcher." Leopardi's concept of *nulla* (or nothingness) as well as his experience of *noia* (an untranslatable term akin to Baudelaire's "ennui") also figure in the poem "The Reader."

"The Italian Muse": Henry James was 26 years old in 1869, the year he first traveled to Rome. He recorded his initial impressions in a series of exultant letters (*Letters 1843–1875*, 1974). His increasingly distilled characterizations of the city appear in a group of travel pieces, most notably *Transatlantic Sketches* (1875) and *Italian Hours* (1909), and in three fictional works with Roman settings: *Roderick Hudson* (1876), "Daisy Miller" (1878), and *The Portrait of a Lady* (1881).

"Orpheus Ascending": In *Labyrinths of Iron* (1981) Benson Bobrick notes that in England a miner sent ahead of the others with an extended flame to burn away accumulated gas was called a *penitent*. The world that Orpheus ascends into resembles mining country everywhere, but especially the English industrial heartland in the second half of the 19th century. I rely upon descriptions of that infernal countryside in autobiographies by John Britton (1850) and James Nasmyth (1883).

"Luminist Paintings at the National Gallery": suggested by the 1980 exhibition at the National Gallery of Art, "American Light: The Luminist Movement, 1850–1875." Hudson River School landscape painters such as Frederic Edwin Church, Fitz Hugh Lane, Martin Johnson Heade and Ralph Blakelock (*The Sun, Serene, Sinks into the Slumberous Sea*) treated light as an in-dwelling of divinity and atmospherics as an embodiment of the American sublime. Emerson's well-known lines come from his 1836 manifesto, "Nature."

"Posthumous Orpheus": Orpheus in the Midwest. In the one letter he wrote from Rome (November 30, 1820), John Keats refers to his own "posthumous existence."

"Art Pepper": Art Pepper (1925–1982) was probably the greatest alto saxophonist in the generation after Charlie Parker. He gives a searing portrait of himself as a junkie, a convict, and a musician in *Straight Life: The Story of Art Pepper* by Art and Laurie Pepper (1979).

"Nebraska, 1883": The nine-year-old girl in this poem resembles Willa Cather at the same age. The italicized lines are adapted from Cather's description of the flat, undulating countryside at the outset of *My Ántonia* (1918).

"Earthly Light": Bob Haak's *The Golden Age: Dutch Painting of the 17th Century* (1984) contains voluminous background information as well as reproductions of most of the paintings invoked. Benjamin Constant's letter to Germaine de Staël about "this brave nation" is quoted by Zbigniew Herbert in *Still Life with a Bridle* (1991). Simone Weil asserts that "absolutely unmixed attention is prayer," in "Attention and Will" (*Gravity and Grace*). George Herbert's phrase "something understood" comes from his poem "Prayer (1)."

A Note About the Author

Edward Hirsch was born in Chicago, in 1950, and educated at Grinnell College and the University of Pennsylvania. His first book of poems, *For the Sleepwalkers* (1981), received the Lavan Younger Poets Award from the Academy of American Poets and the Delmore Schwartz Memorial Award from New York University. His second book of poems, *Wild Gratitude* (1986), received the National Book Critics Circle Award. His third, *The Night Parade*, appeared in 1989. His poems appear frequently in leading magazines and literary periodicals—among them *The Nation*, *The New Republic*, and *The New Yorker*—and he has received a National Endowment for the Arts Fellowship, an Ingram Merrill Award, a Guggenheim Fellowship, and the Rome Prize from the American Academy and Institute of Arts and Letters. He teaches at the University of Houston.

A Note on the Type

This book was set on the Linotype in Granjon, a type named in compliment to Robert Granjon, type cutter and printer in Antwerp, Lyons, Rome, Paris. Granjon, the boldest and most original designer of his time, was one of the first to practice the trade of type founder apart from that of printer.

Linotype Granjon was designed by George W. Jones, who based his drawings on a face used by Claude Garamond (1510–1561) in his beautiful French books. Granjon more closely resembles Garamond's own type than do any of the various modern faces that bear his name.

Composed by Heritage Printers,
Charlotte, North Carolina
Printed and bound by Kingsport Press, Inc.,
Kingsport, Tennessee
Designed by Harry Ford